Nina Hoffmann

LISA D'AMOUR
DETROIT

Lisa D'Amour is a playwright and interdisciplinary artist. She is one half of the Obie Award–winning performance duo PearlDamour, whose work has been presented by the HERE arts center, P.S. 122, the Whitney Museum of Art, the Walker Art Center, and the Fusebox Festival. Her plays have been commissioned and produced by theaters across the country, including the Women's Project, Playwrights Horizons, Clubbed Thumb, New Georges, Salvage Vanguard Theater, Children's Theatre Company, the Kitchen, and Steppenwolf Theatre Company. *Detroit* was a finalist for the 2011 Pulitzer Prize for Drama and the 2011 Susan Smith Blackburn prize. In 2008, D'Amour was awarded the Alpert Award in the Arts in theater. As a playwright, Lisa has received fellowships from the Jerome and McKnight Foundations through the Playwrights' Center, an independent artist commission from the New York State Council on the Arts (for *Stanley [2006]*, created with her brother Todd d'Amour), and an NEA/TCG Theatre Residency (to create *Hide Town* with Infernal Bridegroom Productions). With PearlDamour, she is a three-time recipient of project funding from the Rockefeller MAP Fund and a 2009 Creative Capital grantee. D'Amour received her M.F.A. in playwriting from the University of Texas at Austin and her B.A. in English and Theater from Millsaps College in Jackson, Mississippi. She is a core member of the Playwrights' Center and an alumna of New Dramatists. She lives with her husband, the composer Brendan Connelly, in Brooklyn and New Orleans.

DETROIT

DETROIT

A PLAY BY

LISA D'AMOUR

ff

FABER AND FABER, INC.

AN AFFILIATE OF FARRAR, STRAUS AND GIROUX

NEW YORK

Faber and Faber, Inc.
An affiliate of Farrar, Straus and Giroux
18 West 18th Street, New York 10011

Printed in the United States of America
First edition, 2011

Library of Congress Cataloging-in-Publication Data
D'Amour, Lisa, 1969–
    Detroit : a play / Lisa D'Amour.
        p.   cm.
    ISBN 978-0-86547-865-7 (pbk.)
    1. Suburbs—Michigan—Detroit—Drama.   2. Cities and towns—
United States—Drama.   3. United States—Social conditions—Drama.
I. Title.

PS3604.A43975D48 2011
812'.6—dc22

                                                                2011024874

Designed by Jonathan D. Lippincott

www.fsgbooks.com

5   7   9   10   8   6

Plywood has a lifespan of forty years. Over time, the glue that holds plywood together dries up. Then, walls buckle, split and peel. Panels pop loose. Rooms, doors and windows morph into trick-or-treat versions of themselves.
—Herbert Muschamp, *The New York Times*,
October 19, 1997

Dogs, by this same logic, bark what they cannot understand.
—Heraclitus

ACKNOWLEDGMENTS

Detroit came into being thanks to the devoted ensemble and team of administrators at the Steppenwolf Theatre Company. Thank you to Martha Lavey, David Hawkanson, and their superstar staff for steering the ship. And to the gifted ensemble of Laurie Metcalf, Ian Barford, Kate Arrington, Kevin Anderson, and Robert Breuler. To Austin Pendleton for his wise and sneaky directorial eye. To Polly Carl for introducing my work to Steppenwolf and guiding me through my first production there. And to the Mellon Foundation for helping Steppenwolf bring new plays to life.

While *Detroit* was developed solely at Steppenwolf, the other plays that got me there would have never come into being without the help of these extraordinary theaters and development organizations: New Dramatists, the Playwrights' Center, Clubbed Thumb, the HERE arts center, ArtSpot Productions, and Voice & Vision Theater. In addition, I would like to thank the other small, fierce theater companies that have produced my plays and help me build a writing life: New Georges, P.S. 122, the Kitchen, Theatre of a Two-Headed Calf, Perishable Theatre, Red Eye Theater, Salvage Vanguard Theater, Catastrophic Theatre, Gas & Electric Arts, and Crowded Fire Theater Company, among others.

And then there are the people who take care of me when I leave the theater. There's my family—Brendan Connelly, my amazing husband; my parents, Tay and Gene D'Amour; my brother Todd; my brother Chris and sister-in-law Shenea. My brave agent, Antje Oegel. The list of writers and mentors who keep me inspired and invigorated would turn this into a two-hundred-page acknowledgment. However, there are several who reach so far back, I can't imagine writing without them. Thank you, Katie Pearl, John Walch, Sherry Kramer, Susan Zeder, Erik Ehn, Mac Wellman, Todd London, Karen Hartman, Kathy Randels, and Anne Kauffman.

DETROIT

The world premiere of *Detroit* was produced at the Steppen-wolf Theatre in Chicago (Austin Pendleton, director; Kevin Depinet, scenic design; Rachel Healy, costume design; Kevin Rigdon, lighting design; Josh Schmidt, sound design and original music; Polly Carl, dramaturg; Tommy Rapley, choreographer; Matt Hawkins, fight choreographer; Michelle Medvin, stage manager; Rose Marie Packer, assistant stage manager; Erica Daniels, casting director; Adam Goldstein, assistant director; Anthony Werner, assistant dramaturg; Gina Patterson, lighting assistant; Brendan Connelly, assistant to the sound designer; Joann White, charge scenic artist; Melissa Rutherford, assistant change artist; Emily Guthrie, properties overhire; Kelly Crook, stage management apprentice; Andrew Berg, John Ginter, Christopher Grubb, carpenters; Emily Altman, Zoe Shiffrin, painters). The first performance was on September 9, 2010.

BEN	Ian Barford
MARY	Laurie Metcalf
KENNY	Kevin Anderson
SHARON	Kate Arrington
FRANK	Robert Breuler

CHARACTERS

BEN, raised in the United States, somewhere inland: Kansas City, maybe Denver; worked at one bank for five years and another bank for six years; recently laid off from his job

MARY, raised in the United States, somewhere inland: Kansas City, maybe Denver; met Ben after college at an after-work happy hour; works as a paralegal at a small to midsize law firm

KENNY, raised in several cities in California until he was twelve or thirteen and his parents finally split up and he moved to Omaha with his mom; now works as a warehouse manager; fresh out of major substance abuse rehab

SHARON, raised in Tucson, Arizona, until she was nine; then she and her mother moved to Columbus, Ohio, for two years and then to Indianapolis, where she went to high school; in her junior year her mother moved back to Arizona with her boyfriend, and Sharon lived with her best friend to finish school; now works at a phone bank, answering customer service calls; fresh out of major substance abuse rehab

FRANK, two generations older than the other characters; maybe in his late seventies, early eighties, but he's spry, the kind of man who's been fixing his roof and rewiring the electricity on his house and taking care of his impeccable lawn for many years; he's happy

PLACE

Not necessarily Detroit. However, we are in a "first ring" suburb outside of a midsize American city. These are the suburbs that comprise the first "ring" of houses outside the city proper. They were built in the late 1950s, smaller houses of outdated design. The kind of house many people today would consider a "starter house," or a house you would want to purchase, live in, and keep your eye on the lot next door so you could buy that, knock both houses down, and build a double-lot house.

TIME

Now.

SET NOTE

This play is set in the front yards and backyards of the characters' houses. *Detroit* can also be set in just the backyards of the two houses—see the addendum at the end of the script for the line changes necessary to make this work. In the initial production at Steppenwolf, the show was produced with two backyards, side by side, visible throughout the show.

CASTING NOTE

When I wrote the play, I imagined Mary, Ben, Sharon, and Kenny to be around thirty-four years old. I've since realized that there is some flexibility in terms of the ages of the characters. For example, the show can be cast with Mary and Ben a little older, in their forties, and Sharon and Kenny younger, in their late twenties or early thirties. It's also possible that Kenny is quite a bit older than Sharon. I just ask that directors consider how the age of the characters reverberates through the whole script: the focus of the story can shift quite a bit depending on how old they are.

SCENE 1

Lights Up.

SHARON *and* KENNY *are in* MARY *and* BEN*'s backyard. They sit in newish-looking lawn chairs—part of a set from somewhere like Home Depot.* MARY *struggles to get a patio umbrella to go up as she speaks. It's in the middle of the table and it's heavy. There is a grill nearby.*

MARY And the man with the birthmark looked up and slid a handwritten receipt across the table to me. He said, "Is there anything else I can help you with?" and I said no thank you and I turned and walked out onto the wooden pier and I saw a very old seagull swoop down into the water and eat a fish.

SHARON How did you know it was old?

MARY I just knew.

KENNY And the bank was an old card table on the edge of an abandoned boardwalk?

MARY And all the deposits went into an Adidas shoebox the banker kept under the table.

SHARON They make those shoes in Germany. I went there

7

for a week on this high school trip and everyone wanted to buy them. We all thought they were cheaper over there. I didn't buy any.

MARY (*under her breath*) Shit. Shit shit shit.

KENNY Can I help you with that?

MARY No. I'll be right back.

MARY *goes inside.* KENNY *and* SHARON *sit in the chairs in silence. They hardly even look at each other. The sounds we hear: birds. A lawn mower in the distance. A clanging sound, like someone fixing something. A siren that we hear and quickly fades.* MARY *comes out with* BEN *following her.* BEN *has a pan full of meat, some kind of steaks.* MARY *is kind of in a tizzy.*

MARY I hold it up and I press the button, but nothing works. Sometimes it stays for like two seconds, but then it falls down again.

BEN *fools with the umbrella. They all watch. He pulls his hands away. The umbrella stays up. Pause.*

BEN Wa-lah.

SHARON *laughs just a couple of laughs. No one else laughs.*

MARY It's funny, when you first moved in, we didn't know if anyone was actually living next door. Ben swore he saw someone coming and going. But at weird times. And the sheets stayed up for so long it still looked empty. It was driving him crazy! So when I saw you yesterday morning, I knew I had to grab you and tell

you that we didn't know you were there, that's why
we didn't stop by to say hello.

SHARON We're still not totally moved in. The house belongs
to his aunt.

KENNY Belonged to my aunt. She passed away.

MARY Oh, that was your aunt?

KENNY We're renting it for a while before they sell.

SHARON We'll probably buy it, though.

BEN That's the way to do it, from a friend or family member.
You can avoid a lot of closing costs.

KENNY That's what they say.

SHARON So yes, it's a new start! I mean, we don't have any
furniture even!

MARY Oh, everybody says that—"We don't have any furniture."

KENNY Well—

BEN There are some good outlet stores over on 265. That's
where I got my TV chair.

MARY Oh wait. I've got something!

MARY *goes inside. She has a little trouble with the sliding glass door.
She is just inside the house, so she can call back to the group.*

SHARON Such a great backyard.

MARY *(calling from inside)* Isn't it great?

BEN Thanks, we love it. It sold us on the neighborhood.

SHARON Hey, who is the woman who jogs around the neighborhood in the hot pink jogging outfit?

MARY What?

SHARON Who is the woman who jogs around the neighborhood in the hot pink jogging outfit?

MARY I don't know. I've never seen her. Ben, have you seen this woman? Jogging?

BEN No, I don't think so. There are a lot of people jogging in the morning.

SHARON This one wears a hot pink jogging suit.

MARY *is back at the door, carrying a coffee table, trying to get it through the door.*

MARY I don't know. I don't know who that is.

KENNY Wait, wait let me help.

MARY Oh god, this door!

KENNY Hold on, I've got it. I've got it.

KENNY *brings the coffee table through the door. It is an older model, kind of heavy and clunky, possibly with a glass top.* MARY *puts the coffee table down in front of* SHARON.

MARY This is for you.

SHARON What?

MARY You said you didn't have any furniture. So this is for you.

BEN Honey, that's our coffee table.

MARY I hate this coffee table. Do you like it?

KENNY Uh, yeah, it's nice. Do you like it?

MARY I mean, it's a good coffee table. It's very sturdy. I think it will be good for you. I just—

SHARON I love it. (*pause*) Thank you.

MARY It's for you.

SHARON I know. It's amazing.

SHARON *half touches the coffee table.*

MARY Now Ben has to buy me a new table! Ha-ha!
BEN Ha-ha.

SHARON *sits and indicates the coffee table to* KENNY, *like "nice, table right?"* BEN *speaks kind of loud.*

BEN All right, everybody. I'm going to throw these puppies on the grill!
KENNY (*To* SHARON. *If* MARY *hears it, she pretends not to*) Can you imagine if they really were puppies?

SHARON *and* KENNY *giggle at their private joke.* MARY *speaks to* BEN.

MARY Did you do the marinade? (*she takes a step, and something hurts in her foot*) Ow!

SHARON *half gets up from her chair.*

SHARON Are you okay?
MARY Yes, no. Ow. It's fine, I just have this, well, I have this oh god plantars wart in the bottom of my foot. God, so embarrassing, but do you know what that is? This is a really nasty, yes, wart that grows upward, *into* your foot, slowly, so it takes you a while to notice it, and when you finally do, it hurts hurts hurts and you try to put that drugstore wart remover stuff on it and it won't work, and so you go to the doctor—I went to the doc-

11

tor, I went to the doctor today—and he said he could cut it out, but he would have to inject anesthesia into my foot and then do minor surgery—I know—and since I knew you all were coming over, I thought it would be best to wait, so I'm having it done next Thursday and just making do until then. It is only when I step a certain way . . . it must hit a nerve or something.

KENNY Like when you have a cavity?

SHARON Oh right, and you bite down on ice or something soft like an apple that goes way up?

KENNY Or like a caramel candy.

MARY And start chewing everything supercautiously, like half chewing because you're afraid of that zap and then one day you forget and you bite regular—

Everybody kind of groans and cringes.

BEN Okay okay, let's not—eew—now you've given me the creeps.

KENNY Let's talk about something else.

MARY Yes, let's. Sorry, let's.

BEN So where do you guys work?

KENNY I work in a warehouse over off of 694.

SHARON I work in a phone bank. Is that what you call it? It's like customer service. I sit in one of the booths, take the calls, and either give people answers or send them on to the supervisor.

MARY Oh that sounds interesting.

SHARON Really?

MARY I work as a paralegal at Furley, Clark and Lamb.

KENNY What do you do, Ben?

BEN Ha-ha. I'm a deadbeat. No but really, I got laid off my job at this bank. I was a loan officer, and they like laid everybody off like literally. I don't know who is doing the work anymore. And so they gave me this like half-way decent severance pay and also I could get unemployment, so I am using it as an opportunity to set up my own business.

MARY He's home all day.

BEN It's a financial planning business. Helping people with their credit scores, that sort of thing.

SHARON Ha! We could use that help!

BEN You and a lot of people. It can slip so fast.

SHARON And then you can't get it back up again.

BEN Well, there are strategies, but it takes a lot of patience. We can have a session sometime.

SHARON That would be great.

BEN I need to practice on people. You all can be my test case. And then when you're hanging out on your private yacht, I can use a quote from you on my website.

SHARON Sounds good to me!

MARY He's designing a website. The whole business is going to be run right inside of it.

BEN I'm building it myself, to save money.

MARY He's got this great book, and it talks a lot about breathing deep and taking your time.

SHARON Uh-huh.

BEN And how important it is to spend a lot of time doing things you're passionate about. If you follow your passions, you're halfway there.

MARY If you panic and start to cut corners, then forget it, it's like building a house on quicksand.

BEN It's really all about envisioning your life as financially sound.

MARY It's scary, but I really think it's true. It's a great book.

KENNY Oh, so maybe that's why you had that dream?

MARY Dream?

KENNY The one about the bank being a card table at the edge of an abandoned whatchamacallit. With the deposits in the shoebox.

MARY Oh, right.

BEN All right, we gonna eat some meat!

BEN *gets up to check the meat.*

SHARON (*to* BEN) Are you British?

BEN What?

SHARON Are you from England?

BEN No, why?

SHARON I don't know. Something about the way you talk. "Now you've given me the creeps."

BEN "Now you've given me the creeps." I didn't even realize I said it like that. Huh.

SHARON Maybe you're British.

BEN (*kind of laughs, but he doesn't really know what she means*) Yeah, maybe.

We hear the meat sizzling on the grill.

SHARON Wow, steak.

We hear the grill and some surrounding sounds.

BEN Does anyone want a beer?

KENNY and SHARON (*they overlap in their reply*) We don't drink.

MARY (*speaks under her breath*) I told you that, Ben.

Short pause.

BEN Oh well, does anyone need anything? What are you drinking, seltzer?

KENNY I'm okay.

SHARON I'd love a little more ice.

MARY Oh, I'll bring out a bucket.

BEN Mary, these are just going to be a couple more minutes if you want to check the potatoes.

MARY Oh, right.

MARY *goes inside.*

KENNY So this is a nice patio. Was it here when you moved in?

BEN Yes it was. Yeah, it's great.

KENNY I thought maybe you laid it yourself.

BEN No, no. I work in a bank.

KENNY The edges, the way the cement is pulling up from the edges, it looks like a do-it-yourself job.

BEN Really? Is that a problem? I don't think I noticed—

KENNY No, no. It's totally fine, it's just cosmetic. I only noticed because for a little while I was laying concrete, helping a friend with his business, and we did a lot of patios, so I learned a lot about it. But it's fine.

BEN Yeah. I never noticed.

KENNY You have to buy this sealant and put it on at just the right time or the concrete wants to pull away like that. Really though, you're fine.

BEN Maybe you know why our sliding glass door slides so funny.

KENNY Oh well, I—

BEN See, you have to jiggle it like this to get it over the "hump," see? So you start to open it and you have to go—

He jiggles the door. It opens.

BEN And then it opens. It isn't a big deal, but—oh shit, hold on—

BEN *goes over to the grill.* KENNY *checks out the door.*

KENNY Oh yeah, right. Look, it's the track. I think you might just need a whole new track, but later on let me bang on it a bit with a—do you have a rubber mallet?

BEN No, I don't think so.

KENNY I'll get one. I'll get one and I'll bring it over here and I'll bang on it and we'll see. I think I can fix it.

MARY *slides through the door with the ice bucket.*

MARY Excuse me.

KENNY Excuse me.

MARY The potatoes are perfect!

BEN Ditto on the steaks!

SHARON *takes some ice and puts it in her glass and smiles at* MARY.

SHARON This is awesome. It is so awesome. I mean, who
    invites their neighbors over for dinner anymore?
BEN Ha! We don't have any friends.
MARY Ben!
BEN Well.
SHARON Really, though. I mean we've lived in a bunch of
    neighborhoods now—apartments, houses, condos, even
    a hotel for a little while—
KENNY The house we were renting had a sewer leak—
MARY Eew—
SHARON So the landlord had to put us in a hotel. We've lived
    in a lot of places, and never, never did the neighbors
    give us the time of day. Neighbors. I mean why is that
    word still in the dictionary? It's archaic—am I saying
    the right word? Because you don't need to talk to
    your neighbors anymore. I mean does anyone borrow
    a cup of sugar anymore? No. You drive to the twenty-
    four-hour grocery.
        Because you don't want to bother your neighbors.
        And so if you come home from work and you *do*
    see your neighbor, like, getting out of their car or
    calling their kid inside—wait, what am I saying? Kids
    don't play outside anymore, they might get seduced
    by some homicidal drug addict—ahhhh! Anyway, if
    you get home and your neighbor is out setting the
    timer on their watering system, then you look at the
    ground or maybe give a quick wave and run inside.
    Because maybe you had a bad day or maybe you have
    pinkeye or something and you don't want to get too
    close to them. Always an excuse. And when you get
    inside, behind your closed door, quiet in your house,

you make a pact with yourself to talk to them next time, but then things get . . . fucked up . . . oh, sorry. I didn't mean to say that. I apologize—

KENNY She has a sailor mouth.

SHARON I do. I'm working on it, but I just think there is no real communication anymore, real communication about real things, about that steak or that sliding glass door, or yes, I would love some more ice, but here we are, having that sort of communication and it's just so . . . it's so beautiful—

SHARON *starts to cry. Head in hands. A moment or two of just* SHARON *crying, like deep, private weeping.* BEN *and* MARY *look for a moment, then* BEN *busies himself at the grill.* KENNY *gets up.*

KENNY It's okay, sweetie, just—

KENNY *leans over to comfort* SHARON *and WHAM, the patio umbrella comes crashing down, hitting him on the head.*

KENNY *Ow!*

BEN Oh shit.

KENNY *is holding the back of his head.*

SHARON Baby, are you okay?

KENNY Yeah, yeah. It's just—hold on, I gotta sit down. Whoo. I'm seeing stars.

MARY Oh, wait you're bleeding, you're bleeding, let me get a towel.

MARY *races to go inside. She can't get the sliding door open.*

BEN You have to jiggle it jiggle it jiggle it. No, like this—

BEN *runs over and jiggles the door, or does* KENNY *get up and jiggle it with his hand still on his head? Whatever it is, it's mayhem.*

KENNY No, it's okay, really. I'm sure it's just—I just need a
    second—(*He takes his hand away. He really is bleeding*)
    Oh, wait, yeah, maybe a towel.
SHARON Shit, baby, just keep the pressure on—

MARY *runs back out with a towel.*

MARY I can't believe this. Ben, that (*quickly, almost under her
    breath*) goddamned (*back to normal voice*) umbrella!
BEN I know, I know.
KENNY It's okay, it's gonna be fine—
SHARON He's got a hard head, right baby?
KENNY Heh-heh. Maybe a little ice?
SHARON The ice is right here. (*she gets a handful of ice out of the
    bucket and puts it in the towel*)
MARY Ben, let's just take the umbrella out, okay? Like I sug-
    gested yesterday. Because this keeps happening, and I
    didn't want anyone to get hurt. So let's just take the
    thirty seconds—(BEN *slips the umbrella out from the hole
    and leans it against the house*) Yes, the thirty seconds it
    takes to take the umbrella out so no one gets hurt,
    and we can consider a new umbrella that isn't from
    the fucking—excuse me—bargain basement—

BEN Mary—

MARY So that our guests aren't required to get stitches just for daring to come into our backyard.

SHARON It's okay, really—

KENNY I don't need stitches. I've had stitches before.

BEN Where's the tag? I'm calling the manufacturer. In fact, I should call them right now. (SHARON *and* KENNY *are like, no no no no don't worry, really*) Kenny, we can take you to the hospital. (SHARON *and* KENNY *are even more like no no no really*)

BEN Where is that tag—

BEN *realizes something about the situation. He slips outside of his tizzy and returns to calm host mode.*

BEN Okay. Okay, look at us. Look at us. Kenny, you're fine?

KENNY Totally. I'm just going to keep the pressure on for a bit.

BEN All right, then.

SHARON (*in a bad British accent*) Alrighty, then, Ben.

BEN What?

SHARON I said, "Alrighty, ole chap, cup a tea!" You're British! Admit it! Admit it!

KENNY Sharon—

BEN So. How 'bout some steak?

SHARON Let's do it!

BEN *starts taking steaks off the grill.*

BEN Kenny, you get the first one in honor of your concussion.

KENNY Ha-ha.

MARY Potatoes.

SHARON Do you all ever have "twice-baked" potatoes?

BEN Oh yeah, with all that cream in them.

SHARON Yes!

MARY Sometimes, but they are so much work.

SHARON My mom used to make those all the time.

A few moments of sitting down and settling in. BEN *is sitting down, and they are all taking their first bites.*

KENNY Aw yeah. (*he gives* BEN *the thumbs-up*)

MARY Delicious, honey.

Does one of them get a piece of gristle and do that weird chewing thing where you have to get it out of your mouth and spit it in your napkin? BEN *glances over into* KENNY *and* SHARON*'s yard.*

SHARON I can't believe I cried.

MARY Oh, now—

BEN Cried?

SHARON A few minutes ago. When I was talking about neighbors.

BEN God, did I miss that? Did I forget?

SHARON They say it's part of the process, feeling things, letting your emotions just happen in real time rather than running away from them on that glossy motorcade of substances.

MARY Process?

KENNY (*under his breath*) Baby, we were going to keep that to ourselves—

SHARON Kenny and I met in Eldridge Smith Tomforde.

MARY (*gets it*) Oh.

BEN (*Eating. Chipper, oblivious*) What's Eldridge Smith Tomforde?

Pause for a moment.

MARY It's a rehab facility, honey. For substance abuse.

BEN (*still chipper*) Oh, so that's why you don't drink.

KENNY Yes, and that's why we don't smoke crack or shoot crystal meth or snort big fat lines of cocaine at four in the morning for the third day in a row.

Quick pause, then SHARON *starts to laugh. Then* KENNY *laughs and* MARY *sort of smiles.*

BEN Well, more power to you. And so you met in this . . . this . . .

SHARON Facility. Yes. We were both in for three months— we arrived the same week.

KENNY And we resisted the attraction for at least a month.

SHARON Because you're supposed to. You're actually supposed to resist it for a year, but—

KENNY (*re: hot* SHARON) But who can resist this, right?

BEN *and* KENNY *laugh knowingly, but it is a little weird.*

SHARON And it's so strange "getting out." Those doors part and you walk outside into the hot air, thinking about your apartment that's waiting for you, still sealed shut, filled with all your crappy stuff, dishes molding in the sink, countertops piled with old beer cans and underwear and pipes and stuffed animals covered in puke. And you're standing outside the hospital, clutching each other's sweaty hands for dear life—

And then there was this house.

KENNY My aunt died.

SHARON There was this house, and—this is not a lie—we went to T.J.Maxx and I bought a dress with flowers on it and a pair of "flats." "Flats," and Kenny bought a suit—

KENNY It was two hundred and fifty dollars marked down to thirty-four ninety-nine.

SHARON And he bought shoes also, and an undershirt and socks . . .

KENNY And we went to see my great-uncle, who was very close to my aunt. She left the house to him—

SHARON And we asked if we could live here. We asked him to give us a chance.

Blackout.

SCENE 2

The sounds of the neighborhood moving into night:

The hum of air-conditioning units, and air-conditioning units starting up and shutting off, a couple of cars driving by, a car or two parking, doors opening and closing. Perhaps an automatic garage door opening. The faint sound of a few joggers jogging and a few kids riding their bikes.

The car and people sounds begin to fade and are replaced by crickets and a few frogs, still mixed in with the air-conditioning sounds.

And someone is having a fight behind closed doors. Then the sound of "No, no, no, no, NO" as a door opens and the "no's" become louder. The same door slams.

Loud knocking on a door. Knocking and then the sound of MARY *whispering loudly, "Sharon! Sharon! Open up! Shaaaaron!" And more knocking.*

The lights fade up; middle-of-the-night outdoor light. We are in KENNY *and* SHARON's *backyard. Theirs is a very basic brick suburban house. Or it has siding. Some shrubs but no flowers. Really bare-bones. There is one taller potted plant on the porch, a plant that is like a small tree, with some blossoms on it. Other than that, nada.*

MARY *is in her bathrobe, banging on the front door. She is near tears.*

SHARON *opens the door in her T-shirt and underwear.*

SHARON Mary, what's—

MARY *falls into her arms. She weeps outright for maybe five seconds—*

SHARON Mary, can you just—

Another wave of weeping. Eventually MARY *half composes herself. Anytime* MARY *curses she says that word kind of under her breath.*

MARY It's just I don't know how to help him. I'm at the frayed edge of my wits. He gets to be home all day and I don't get home until six forty-five because of the *fucking* traffic on 694, and he's been home all day and I get home and he's already on his first drink. He *says* it's his first drink, anyway. And he's cooked dinner, which is of course very sweet, but then I say something about how his green beans taste different from my green beans— you know, like "oh, these taste different," just like that, not saying anything bad, but he drops his fork and I know he's offended and then it starts. And I hate *NASCAR Unmasked and Personal* and he knows I hate it. I mean, he's not a NASCAR kind of guy. He doesn't like NASCAR, he just likes that show, and he turns it on anyway while I'm finishing my dinner, while I'm washing the dishes, and he watches the TV so fucking loud—even the commercials, and he laughs at commercials, at *dumbfuck* commercials like the one with the cartoon chicken getting rubbed down with chicken magic. (She *imitates the commercial. It is a Latino chicken*) "Ieeee! It tickles!" I mean, Sharon, it's so *fucking crackass* dumb. And so I ask, "How was it today? Did you bring the files to Kinko's?" And he's like, "Oh *shit*. No, I forgot. Oh well, I'll do it tomorrow," and I say, "You know you can do it on their website through the file uploader, its super easy." And he says, "Yes, *yes* I know," and I say, "Well, you know that book you bought for sixty-five dollars said you've got to be hard on yourself about keeping to a schedule. Because Joe Blow down the street is also probably laid off, and also probably about to set up his dream business where you get to sit home all day and tell other people how to clean up the fucking financial wasteland of their day-to-day existence. And if Joe Blow gets his portfolio together before you do, then Joe Blow gets the clients, not you." And he says, "Joe Blow can suck my *nutsack*." (*pause for a moment, that word is like a bad taste in her mouth*) And I say, "Oh, that's a winning attitude." And then that's it—we're fighting and he's all "I'm trying to be proactive" and I'm all "Today sucked, I barely got to eat lunch" and he's all "I'm afraid" and I'm like "Don't say it like that" and he's like "Look, I have to put my beer on the floor! The photo album too!" And I'm like "That coffee table didn't *go* in this *room*—"

SHARON You can have it back—

MARY I don't want it back. I want to live in a tent in the woods. With one pot and one pan. And an old-fashioned aluminum mess kit with its own mesh bag. I want my hair to smell like the smoke from yesterday's fire, when I cooked my fish and my little white potatoes. I want to dry out my underwear on a warm rock. And feel the cold water rushing around my ankles, my feet pressing into the tiny stone bed that holds up the stream. Silver guppies nosing their heads into my calves . . .

Quiet for a moment. We hear suburban wind, perhaps a car passing on another street. Perhaps some teenagers laughing, some kids in the house across the street, listening to music in their room.

SHARON Were you a Girl Scout?
MARY Yes.
SHARON I thought so.

MARY *leans over, or squats down, into the bushes, and pukes. And pukes. She leans back up, wiping her mouth.*

MARY Oh god, my head. I think I need some water.
SHARON Mary, have you ever thought about getting some help?
MARY Some help with what?
SHARON With your drinking problem.

MARY *looks at* SHARON *like she is an alien from another planet.*

MARY I thought I could just come to you and talk.
SHARON You can, you did.
MARY Because you cried at my house and—
SHARON (*simultaneously*) I know.
MARY I thought that was awesome. That you felt comfort-able enough to do that . . . it made me feel like a good host that you felt okay letting go. In that way—

SHARON You are a good host. But you can be a great host and still have a drinking problem.

MARY *gets loud. Too loud for this neighborhood. She no longer quiets her curse words.*

MARY You know what? FUCK YOU. (*she stands up and stumbles a little*) I come over here asking for HELP and what is the FIRST THING YOU FUCKING DO? Accuse me of being a fucking DRUNK? I MEAN IF THAT IS NOT THE BLACK CALLING THE KETTLE POT. God. My husband is offering the two of you his services FOR FREE. He wouldn't even blink to ask for payment. Wouldn't even BLINK. And look at you. This fucking yard.

BEN *walks up. He is obviously not drunk. He is stone-cold sober, and it takes* MARY *a little while to see him.*

MARY There's not even a single FERN. You've made no effort.
SHARON Well, we just moved in—
MARY (MARY *grabs onto* SHARON) I was hiding behind our bushes. I snuck out the door to get some air. I JUST NEEDED SOME AIR. I needed to get out of the house. And he wouldn't let me. He kept locking the door on me. And so when the commercial came on, I snuck out the front door and just squatted there behind the bushes. He called and called. My toes were in the mulch, I was breathing, I was not answering.

Because he doesn't like me, nobody likes me, and I just wanted to breathe.

And then I thought, "Sharon likes me. She cried in my yard."

MARY *hugs* SHARON, *and pukes over* SHARON's *shoulder.* SHARON *has to kind of brush it off her back and the back of her arm.* BEN *catches* MARY. KENNY *opens the door, half asleep, in his boxers.* MARY *notices it's* BEN.

MARY GET AWAY FROM ME! GET HIM AWAY!

BEN *pulls* MARY *to him and speaks to her softly in her ear. She's listening. She's saying these words as he whispers in her ear.*

MARY Uh-huh. Uh-huh. My head is pounding. It's like there's cats inside. I know. I know I'm a good person. I know, Tootsie-Too. Yes. Yes. I want to go home. I want to get in the tub. Ow, my foot.

MARY *is quiet in* BEN's *arms.* BEN *looks at* SHARON *and* KENNY. *Everyone except* MARY *sees someone approaching.* BEN *tries to hold* MARY *up a little better. We hear the sound of footsteps jogging by. All at once* BEN, SHARON, *and* KENNY *give a quick wave, as if they are waving back to someone.*

BEN That's her?
SHARON That's her. How dumb is that, jogging at eleven at night.
KENNY And she'll be back at it at six-thirty.

SHARON Show-off.
KENNY I really need to start exercising again.

Pause for a quick moment as they watch her go.

BEN I'm really—
SHARON and KENNY No, really, it's okay really.
BEN We'll buy you a new shirt—
KENNY Don't worry, please—
SHARON We've been through this—
KENNY Remember?
BEN I'll see you tomorrow, Kenny.
KENNY One-thirty!

BEN *starts to walk* MARY *home.*

BEN Please don't worry about your yard—
MARY (*her foot hurts as she walks*) Ow. *Ow.*
BEN It's going to be a nice yard. I like that new plant.

BEN *and* MARY *are almost to their house.* SHARON *speaks softly.*

SHARON The funny thing is, it's fake.

SHARON *and* KENNY *watch them go for a few seconds. A quick kiss, then they head back inside. Before the door closes—*

Blackout.

SCENE 3

Daytime sounds. Lawn mowers, kids on bikes, a plane overhead, hum of air-conditioner compressors in people's backyards, a couple of birds.

Lights up bright on BEN *and* MARY's *backyard. Are* KENNY *and* SHARON *in almost the same seats they were in the other day? The umbrella is gone and the table is set just a little bit fancier—perhaps a lace doily on the table and some fresh flowers.*

BEN Hey, Kenny, are you building a deck over there?

KENNY Yeah. I'm getting started. That's the foundation you see right there. I'm going to finish the decking in the corner. I can't decide if I want to put up a railing or not.

BEN Well, it's nice for leaning—

KENNY Yeah, but then you have to really reinforce it.

BEN Or if there are kids around, if you want to keep the kids on the deck.

KENNY Yeah, we'll see. (KENNY *smiles at* SHARON) We're just taking it one step at a time.

MARY (*offstage, in the house*) Honey, will you get the door? (BEN *slides the sliding door open for* MARY)

MARY Look how that sliding door just zips open!
BEN Your husband's a genius, Sharon.

KENNY *smiles.* MARY *enters with an enormous tray of hors d'oeuvres beautifully presented. It is a little intimidating how beautifully presented they are. Her foot is bandaged and she is wearing a funny orthopedic sandal on that foot that doesn't let her put pressure on the front of her foot.*

MARY All right, everybody, so we've got some dates wrapped in bacon drizzled with some chili oil, and this is a Danish Havarti that I mashed with some basil and it is really great with this special olive oil— you just need a little. These are slices of "heirloom tomatoes"—do you know what that is? I drove all the way to Whole Foods to get them. They've been grown from the same seed for hundreds of years, meaning the plants grow and drop their seeds and those seeds are used for the next plants. Try that with the olive oil and a little bit of this special pink salt—
KENNY Special salt?
MARY I know, I know, you think, "Salt"—"Salt is salt," right? But here, taste it with a tomato—
KENNY Oh, I don't like tomatoes—
SHARON (*as in: be polite*) Kenny—
MARY Oh well taste it with the Havarti, then. Go ahead, taste it—

She hands him a cracker with Havarti and a bit of salt. They watch him taste it. He chews.

34

KENNY Oh yeah.

MARY See? I was right, right?

KENNY Yeah, it takes a second, but then—wow! (*to* SHARON) Taste this.

SHARON I wish I could cook.

He feeds a bite to SHARON.

MARY Oh, you can cook! It's special pink salt from the bottom of a special river. Ben, what's the name of that river? Ben? And this—(*she holds up a little bowl*) is caviar.

BEN Caviar?

MARY Caviar that came all the way from Norway.

SHARON Wow. Kenny won't even let me buy Dijon mustard.

MARY *hands* SHARON *some caviar on a cracker.*

BEN Where did you buy caviar?

MARY It doesn't matter, Ben.

SHARON Oh it's good!

MARY Right?

BEN (*claps his hands*) Okay, let's throw these puppies on the grill!

MARY Oh Ben, let's wait just a few minutes. I just brought out the appetizers.

BEN Yes, but chicken takes longer.

MARY Let's sit a minute—(*she pulls a patio chair so it is side by side with hers*)

BEN But I—

MARY I know, but let's just relax a minute.

KENNY Come sit, Ben.

SHARON Rest.

Tiny pause.

BEN Okay, all right.

BEN *sits next to* MARY. MARY *grabs his hand and holds it. Smile.*
Pause. SHARON *sings to them, getting the words a bit wrong.*

SHARON "Don't stop believin'. Hold on to that feeeever . . ."
BEN Oh, I love that song.
KENNY Remember MTV?
SHARON It's still on, dummy.
BEN (*singing the next line with wrong words*) "Streetlight, fever . . ."
MARY What about you, Sharon, how's work?
SHARON Oh, you know—
MARY Sure, and you Kenny?
KENNY You know, it's a job.
BEN You've just got to reach the one-year mark.
KENNY One solid year with the same job and same address.
　　　Then everything starts to open up—
MARY Like a good bottle of wine.
BEN (*to* SHARON) We had a great session.
SHARON He told me. So Ben, is it true you're a NASCAR
　　　man?
BEN (*laughs*) No, no. I just like the show, that behind-the-
　　　scenes show. It's just brain drain, you know. The driv-
　　　ers and their trophies. And their trophy wives. A good
　　　way to decompress. I barely have to pay attention.
MARY One time I watched a whole episode of *Fit to Be Tied*,
　　　and when it got to the end, I realized that I hadn't
　　　really seen any of it.

SHARON Yes!

MARY I was thinking about something else the whole time . . . stewing about something . . . and so to Ben it looked like I was watching the show, but really I was on another planet . . . a really angry planet.

KENNY That sounds like the last five years of my life.

SHARON Up until now, right?

KENNY Sure thing, hotpants.

BEN (*laughing a little*) Hotpants—

SHARON I like *How Far Will You Go for Your Man?*

BEN Oh, what's that one?

SHARON There are all these boyfriend-girlfriend teams, and the man asks the girl to do things . . . sometimes simple things, like give him a bath and rub him with hot oil, and other times it's like crazy, like three ways or four ways. And the girl that will go the farthest for her man gets one point five million dollars.

MARY Is that like on the Playboy Channel or something?

SHARON I don't know. Our house came with magic cable.

KENNY It was just there when we screwed it into the TV.

SHARON It all just gets piped in from somewhere out in the cosmos.

KENNY There's this one channel that is just a picture of this satellite dish on top of a building. I think it is a hospital. And the satellite is facing out—so you really just see the back of it. And there is this voice reading from some kind of manual . . . I think it is maybe instructions to work the satellite dish? It's hard to tell. And that's all the channel shows.

SHARON Why do you watch that channel?

KENNY I don't really watch it.

SHARON Well then, what are you doing when you stare at it?

BEN I think I'll put the meat on.

KENNY You need help?

BEN (*motions: "no, no sit"*) All I want in the whole world is a meat thermometer. Mary, can we get a meat thermometer?

MARY After we make our first million from your website, ha-ha.

KENNY Hey Mary, how's your foot?

MARY Oh it's good! The thing took like twenty minutes. The worst part was the shot. The doctor stuck the needle into the arch of my foot, and I could feel it shoot all the way up through my stomach and heart and throat and into my eyeball.

BEN I've never heard her yell like that.

MARY But then everything went dead and the doctor could just dig right in.

KENNY Eew.

SHARON That's good that it's better.

MARY This shoe helps a lot, actually.

SHARON See, Mary went to the doctor and it was fine. Kenny's afraid of the doctor.

KENNY I'm working on it.

MARY Kenny, do you want to try some caviar?

KENNY The funny thing is, I'm allergic.

MARY To caviar?

SHARON He puffs up instantly. We were in the VIP section in this club in Atlanta, and they had all this fancy shit. Excuse me, this fancy food. And we were, well, we were high as kites and just eating and eating, and all of a sudden he was on the floor, his eyes turning black, his whole face getting puffier and puffier.

KENNY I couldn't breathe.

SHARON They called an ambulance.

KENNY Which sucked because I didn't have insurance.

SHARON Three days in the hospital. I slept there. He woke up with night sweats. The doctor said if I ever eat caviar, I should brush my teeth because if I kiss him, especially if I tongue kiss him, he could just blow up again. Like a blowfish. He's that allergic.

KENNY It was crazy. That was like eight years ago. I've avoided caviar ever since.

MARY But wait—I thought you met in rehab.

KENNY Oh, that's a funny story.

MARY What do you mean?

SHARON We *did* meet in rehab, but we just realized a couple weeks ago that we had met before. In Hotlanta. And we had that adventure together. I actually snuck out of the hospital while he was asleep and got on a bus to Chi-town. Chicago. I mean I hardly knew him then. I mean we were a mess.

KENNY I think we both just erased Hotlanta from our minds. What was the name of that club?

SHARON Who knows? Razoo. Numbers. Buzz Buzz.

KENNY The Compound. Third Base.

SHARON Ampersand.

KENNY Pirate Dan's. (SHARON *kind of chuckles a bit.* KENNY *does too. It's a private moment*) Hotlanta was *fucked up*, yo.

MARY (*picks up a pitcher*) Lemon ginger iced tea?

SHARON Why, thank you, I would love some lemon ginger iced tea. You guys have to come over. Soon. I mean look at that, the yard is right there. I could spit and hit it. Watch, I'm going to spit. (*she spits and hits the yard*)

KENNY Yes, let's make that happen. As soon as the deck is finished.

SHARON Fuck the deck! Oh, sorry. I mean fart on the deck! These are our neighbors, Kenny. We've lived here almost five weeks. We've got to have our neighbors over. We've got to fight against the anonimater . . . anonyminimous . . .

MARY and BEN (*staggered, trying to help her with the word*) Anonymity?

SHARON Yes! We've got to fight that. I mean, everywhere else we lived we hid from our neighbors and they hid from us, because nobody wanted to interact with us *ever*. I mean they knew, they could see. And they could just ignore us—la la la la la—that's your space, this is mine, no I don't hear the screams and moans of a drug addict. No, I don't see those junkie friends with blood caked in their hair la la, that's your space. Dust your hands, shoot the rooster in the foot, and be done with it.

But things are different now. We can have company. We can have a nice time.

MARY Of course you can.

SHARON Tomorrow. Come over tomorrow.

KENNY Sharon, there's nowhere to sit!

SHARON We'll figure it out. Mary and Ben, would you like to come to our house for dinner tomorrow?

40

KENNY It's not our house.

SHARON Shut up. Will you? Come over? Will you let us make you dinner at our place? Tomorrow?

BEN (*singing*) "Streetlight, fever . . ."

MARY Ben. I mean Ben, do we have plans?

BEN Sure, I mean no. No plans.

MARY That would be lovely.

SHARON *is excited but also kind of freaked out, as she really does not have the skills or money to pull off this sort of thing.*

SHARON Awesome. Great. Fun. All right. Dinner at our place. Fantastic. (*she spins around in one circle*) Really, super fun!

Blackout.

SCENE 4

Outdoor sounds again, the next day.

    When the lights come up, we are in KENNY *and* SHARON*'s backyard. The deck is half finished, the floor is only three-quarters put down, and most of the boards are loose.* BEN *and* MARY *sit in super crappy folding chairs that really look secondhand—as if* SHARON *and* KENNY *got them out of the basement. There is also an old-fashioned card table with one joint taped up with duct tape.* SHARON *is sitting on an upturned plastic milk crate. Maybe* KENNY *will sit on a couple of bags of charcoal? Or maybe a suitcase? The grill is from the Dollar General. There is a plastic pot of plastic flowers on the card table.*

    KENNY *is working the grill.* SHARON *relates a dream.*

SHARON And I was wandering around inside this strange house. But I knew the house was inside of another house. A house inside a house. I could feel the two houses. And there were these rubber walls, you could press your hand right into them. And I was walking through the house and thinking, "I've got to get this caviar to Mary." (MARY *laughs*) But I knew that Kenny was allergic to caviar and so I didn't want to touch it, so I built this contraption out of chopsticks? To carry the caviar, and I hooked it around my waist right—(*she indicates her abdomen*)

MARY Oh my god, do you think you're pregnant?

SHARON *No.* Definitely no. God, no. So I opened this door in the hallway and inside on this fancy bed was the lady in the pink jogging suit getting the shit fucked out of her by some guy—

KENNY Sharon!

SHARON (*she lifts her hand to her mouth quickly*) Oh god. Shit, I didn't mean that.

BEN Well, that's what was happening. In the dream.

SHARON I know. I'm just trying to work on my language. Can I finish it? The dream? (BEN *and* MARY *are like "sure, sure"*) So I closed the door on her and then I was in the supermarket, the one I used to go to when I was a kid. And I was with Ben, but Ben wasn't Ben. He was this short guy, maybe five feet tall, with this really bad brown dye job on his hair and his beard, and he may have been a leprechaun, but I knew it was Ben and I knew he was *starving* and I had to buy him food. And I would put food in the cart and check my purse for money, but the amount of money I had kept changing, so I would put back the tomatoes and put in maybe green beans because they were cheaper, and I would check my purse and not have enough money and put stuff back, and so on and so on—And I knew I had to feed Ben, he was shriveling, getting smaller, he was sitting in the child's seat of the shopping cart by then.

And then we were at the butcher counter and I

picked Ben up and went behind the counter into the meat locker back there. I sat Ben down on an icy side of beef and he smiled at me, and the butcher came by, looked in, and closed the door right on us. It was cold and I could feel the frost on my face. I tried to form words—I tried to say "Ben, Ben get the door open, we're going to die!" But it just came out like "Buuuh—Buuuh" and then Ben scratched his little beard and put his hand on my hand and I got this intense wave of peace. Radiating through me, like when a tab of ecstasy hits, and I thought, "Oh, I'm dying," but it was so amazing, this feeling of sadness and happiness coming from inside and radiating out, like what bleeding to death must feel like, and then Ben said, in a British accent—

BEN (*Speaks in a British accent. It's a pretty good one. Does he touch* SHARON's *hand as well?*) "When I look at you, I see nothing but becoming."

MARY (*kind of freezes*) Wha— (SHARON *smiles.* MARY *is a little freaked*)

MARY I—I—I think I'm—

BEN (*still in a British accent*) Well, I was in the dream, wasn't I? (*Short pause. Then* BEN *and* SHARON *start laughing*)

SHARON No, no. I already told him the dream—

MARY Oh.

BEN She told me before you came over.

KENNY That was a good accent, Ben!

BEN (*in a British accent*) Not bad there, chap, eh?

SHARON See? It's in there somewhere . . . (SHARON *kind of tickles* BEN *like the Pillsbury Doughboy*)

MARY That was . . . weird . . .

SHARON That was my dream. And I think it was my closure dream. I think I'm better now. Kenny, I'm completely healed.

MARY I'm going inside. Sharon, did you put the vodka inside?

SHARON It's on the counter.

MARY And may I use your bathroom?

SHARON Sure, you'll see it. Right there in the hallway.

MARY *goes inside* KENNY *and* SHARON's *house.* KENNY *claps his hands together.*

KENNY All right, let's throw these puppies on the grill!

SHARON Hey, Ben, I figured out the other day that all the streets around here are named for different kinds of light. We're on Sunshine Way, and then there's Ultraviolet Lane and Fluorescent Avenue.

KENNY Also Rainbow Road.

BEN Yes, *and* did you also notice Feather Boulevard . . . Weightless Avenue . . .

KENNY (*getting it*) Oooh, right—Helium Street . . .

SHARON Uhhhh . . .

BEN "Light" and "light."

SHARON (*gets it*) Oooooooh!

KENNY Weird, right?

SHARON Totally weird.

BEN They planned it that way back in the fifties, I think. If you go to the corner of Sunshine and Route Twenty, there is this big brick sign that fell backward a long time ago . . . Twenty years ago? It's all overgrown with weeds and ivy. But if you peel some of it away,

you can see the original engraved sign: "Bright Houses.
Come to the Light."

KENNY How'd you find that?

BEN I had a friend who lived here when I was in high school.
We were just messing around.

KENNY It's still there?

BEN I think so.

Weird beat. Will the conversation shift?

SHARON Oh shit! I forgot the appetizers.

BEN That's okay.

SHARON No. They're just inside. I'll be right back.

SHARON *goes inside.* BEN *goes up to the deck, kind of "testing" it.*

KENNY Hey man, thanks again for all the advice.

BEN Oh, it's not me, it's the book.

KENNY Yeah, but I never would have read that book.

BEN I'm glad it helped. The deck's sure coming along.

KENNY Yeah, it's gonna be nice. We should sit down again
sometime soon.

BEN Sure thing. (*he looks at the grill*) What is it, burgers?

KENNY Yes, with a ball of American cheese inside. It melts
while it cooks.

BEN (*as in, shit yeah*) Yeah.

KENNY You have to be careful though, you'll burn your
mouth. Hold on I need some salt. (*he moves toward the
house*) You need anything?

BEN Maybe another beer.

KENNY You got it.

KENNY *goes inside as* MARY *comes out. She has a very big plastic cup of vodka tonic.* MARY *goes to Ben, speaking with her voice a little hushed.*

MARY Ben, there's nothing in there.

BEN What?

MARY They've lived here five weeks. And there is no furniture in there. Nothing. Except the coffee table we gave them and this one armchair with stuffing coming out of it. It looks like a dog ate it. And a tiny TV sitting on a cardboard box . . .

BEN Well, they said they had no furniture.

MARY Yes, but *no furniture.*

BEN They're starting from scratch.

MARY And I think there is a smell. Like a bad carpet smell. Like a sick carpet smell.

BEN Oh, come on.

MARY Even the bedroom— (*she takes a big gulp of vodka tonic*)

BEN You went in their bedroom?

MARY There's not even a bed. I mean, there is this mattress-looking thing, and some sheets hanging off it onto the floor, and that T.J.Maxx suit hanging like a carcass in the closet.

BEN You looked in the closet?

MARY I don't know it just makes me feel strange. I mean, who are we talking to?

BEN They're getting it together. I'm sure they have no credit cards, no nothing. I don't even know how he bought this lumber.

MARY They did buy curtains.

BEN Only for the front, did you notice?

MARY Well. They're trying to be good neighbors, I guess.

BEN I don't know, I think they're great. And Kenny's got a good game plan now.

MARY No furniture, no clothes.

BEN Mary, will you just shut up about it? You're being judgmental. How much vodka is in there?

MARY It's not yours.

BEN I can smell it over here.

MARY It's just strange. I feel strange.

KENNY *enters.*

KENNY Ladies and gentlemen, drumroll please!

KENNY *holds the door open.* SHARON *enters with a rusty cookie sheet with some snacks on it.*

SHARON All right so you all the theme is white trash, because I'm trying to own up to what I am these days, ha-ha, and anyway the Cheetos are always the first things to go at a party, right? Even when they're sitting right next to the Brie. *So*, we've got Cheetos, saltines, a canned bean dip, and Cheez Whiz, and then I made Delta caviar—ha-ha no really, it's like anticaviar, so we don't kill Kenny. It's got a can of corn, red peppers and yellow peppers, a can of black-eyed peas, and some Italian dressing—and salt. At least we can afford salt! Wait till you taste it!

BEN I have a weakness for the bean dip. (*he digs in*)

SHARON Mary, try some.

MARY I'll have a Cheeto.

MARY *takes one Cheeto.* KENNY *returns with* BEN's *beer and goes to the grill.*

BEN God, it's so nice to just chill out like this. When I started working from home, I imagined myself totally relaxed, working a couple hours, going for a jog, doing a little gardening—

MARY You don't garden—

BEN I know, I just imagined it. But instead my days are so hectic. I'm always on the phone or trying to learn HTML for my website—

SHARON Ha ask Kenny about trying to learn HTML—

KENNY HTML can kiss my sweet, ripe ass—

BEN Running to *Staples*—Jesus Christ, how many times a day can a man go to Staples! Anyway, I am totally fried by the time Mary comes home and kind of panicky because I feel like I didn't get enough done.

KENNY When do you "launch"?

BEN Well, it was supposed to be this past Monday. But everything always takes longer than you think.

MARY I still don't understand how *just a website* is going to attract customers. I mean it is just hanging out there in the ether. Is someone just going to decide they need a consultant and then—*poof*—find your website?

BEN I've got it, baby—

MARY No, I just mean there are like what, a gazillion bazillion websites out there—

BEN I've got it.

SHARON Anyway, I heard the "next Internet" is coming out soon. Something that we can't even imagine. This superfast thing that will change everything. Change everything so much that like we won't even have to own things anymore.

BEN Do you mean—I don't understand. I mean, what will happen to websites? I don't understand.

SHARON That's just it. I can't explain it, and it's outside of our understanding at this time—

BEN I mean I'm sure there'll be some sort of conversion, a way to convert the website into—

SHARON Ben. No worries. Our tiny brains can't conceive of it, it's totally new, like finding out . . . this table is actually alive, and has been for a long time. We can't understand it yet, but the inventors of the "next Internet" are doing that part for us. So you, Ben, should just unfurrow—is that a word? Unfurrow that forehead and enjoy some bean dip and Delta caviar.

The distant sound of SHARON *and* KENNY's *doorbell.* SHARON *looks puzzled.*

SHARON Is that our doorbell?

Everyone pauses, listens. Ambient sounds of the neighborhood. Are they the same as usual or have they changed? A moment. Another moment. Another doorbell.

MARY I think it is.

SHARON Who on earth can be ringing our doorbell?

KENNY Do you want me to get it?

SHARON No, you finish the burgers.

Sharon exits.

KENNY Okay, two minutes. (*he yells to* SHARON) HEY SHARON, WHEN YOU COME OUT, BRING THE BUNS AND THE KETCHUP AND STUFF!
    She also made potato salad. She makes awesome potato salad.

MARY I wonder why it was a meat locker.

KENNY What?

MARY In the dream.

KENNY Oh. Who knows?

MARY (*she might say the next line in a British accent*) Ben, would you get me another drink?

BEN No. (MARY *kind of pouts.* KENNY *turns back to the grill*) I'll get you Seven-Up. I'll get you Seven-Up if you want it. Mary, will you please let me get you a Seven-Up?

MARY (*kind of clicks her tongue and sighs*) Sure, all right. (*She hands* BEN *her cup.* BEN *gets up and starts to go toward the house*)

KENNY Hey Mary, Sharon was asking about those plastic plates you have—

Suddenly BEN *falls through one of the boards of the porch. Either it breaks or there was like a slot that his foot could slide through. He falls one or two feet into the porch and catches himself with his hand.*

52

BEN SHIT!

KENNY Oh god—(*goes to help him*)

BEN Ow ow ow SHIT!

MARY Is it broken?

BEN The porch?

MARY No your leg, you *fucking* imbecile.

KENNY Let me help you.

BEN I think it's bleeding, ow OW. Wait, take it slow, shit . . . ahhh . . .

BEN *is now sitting on the porch. His leg has a deep scratch or gash from the wood.*

KENNY I'm getting some ice and water, don't move. Are you sure it's not broken?

BEN No, no I don't think so.

KENNY *runs inside.*

MARY *Fuckwad.*

BEN It wasn't me. It was the porch. The porch isn't finished.

MARY That new Internet is going to come, and then where will we be?

KENNY *comes running out with a cup of water and some ice and a paper towel.*

KENNY Man, this was totally my fault, man. SHIT. Hold on, let's pour some water in it to clean it out—

KENNY *pours water on the wound. It hurts.*

BEN Ow! Ow! This is so dumb!

KENNY I think there are splinters in there. I think we need to pull them out with a tweezer.

BEN Give me a second, man. Just give me a second.

KENNY Aw, man, do you have insurance?

MARY Maybe hydrogen peroxide.

BEN Just give me a second.

We hear SHARON *yelling at someone from inside the house.*

SHARON Yeah, you too, you fucking nutcase! You're a fucking stinky cunt, you hear me? You are insane!

SHARON *enters carrying buns, a bottle of ketchup, a jar of mustard, and a jar of hamburger dill slices. It is a little awkward. She is furious. At some point during this tirade* MARY *slips into the house for some more vodka. Also at some point* SHARON *puts down the buns and the condiments. By the end of the tirade* MARY *is back outside.*

SHARON Kenny you are not going to believe this. I am fucking losing it—do you see me? I am losing it! It was the pink jogging suit lady. At our door! Only she wasn't wearing a pink jogging suit, she was wearing shorts and a blue T-shirt. And she came over to ask us politely—sort of—politely if we could keep our dog from shitting on her lawn.

KENNY We don't have a dog.

SHARON WE DON'T HAVE A DOG. Exactly. And so I said to her, politely, I said, "We don't have a dog" and she said, "Yes you *do* have a dog and it is quite fond of taking craps on my lawn." "Quite fond." Like slicing a razor blade across my face—"quite fond." And I said, "Lady, do you want to come in my house? We've got NOTHING in our house, especially a DOG. Especially we do not have a DOG." And she said, "Listen, missy." FUCKING MISSY! "Listen, missy. I've lived in this neighborhood for six years, and I jog every morning. This dog appeared out of nowhere and started crapping on my lawn. I'm not asking you to get rid of it, I'm just asking you to clean up his crap." And I practically started crying—look at me I'm crying now—and I said, "Ma'am, people have accused me of many things before, but they have never accused me of having a dog. You need to investigate further, you need to knock on other doors—" And she said—her voice changed and she said, "Look, if it craps on my lawn one more time, I am calling the police" and I said, "Are you kidding? The police are going to fucking LAUGH IN YOUR FACE if you call them about some dogshit." And she said, "AHA! So you DO have a DOG!" And I said, "No, no, no, no, no fucking NO there is no dog here, lady!" And she just shook her head and kind of kicked our plant and said, "Ha, I thought it was fake." And turned around. I mean FUCK, Kenny, FUCK. This is like FUCKED UP. (SHARON *sees* BEN) What the fuck happened?

KENNY He fell through the porch.

SHARON Fuck.

MARY It's his own fault.

BEN Can someone get me a wet towel? These paper towels are going to stick.

SHARON Oh, um, yeah, um—(*she starts turning in circles*) Oh wait also the potato salad.

KENNY We only have one towel and I really think it is too dirty to put on your cut.

SHARON I mean what kind of neighborhood have we moved into!

BEN I think we have—Mary, can you—

MARY Maybe we should move to the woods.

KENNY Oh shit the burgers, just a second.

KENNY *goes to the burgers.* BEN *tries to pull a splinter out.* SHARON *looks at* MARY.

BEN Ow.

SHARON Yes, that's it. I'm moving to the woods with my friend Mary. With chipmunks and baby deer for neighbors. Fuck this bullshit place. Where nobody likes you and you get fired from your job because you went back to your car to get your weight-lifting belt.

BEN You got fired from your job? Kenny?

KENNY Baby, can we not—

SHARON It's a fucking crack of shit, crock of shit. And I thank the pink jogging suit lady for helping me see the light of day.

MARY In the woods we could eat rabbits, and if hunting was hard we could eat grasshoppers.

SHARON And we can put a spout into the tree to get the

maple syrup out. Do you know how to do that, Mary?

MARY Sure. And just like you said, No men, baby, no men, just you and me in our tent with our fucking mess kits in the mesh bag and the one pot and the one pan—

SHARON And the sunsets—shit, there will be sunsets!

MARY And no phones.

KENNY The burgers are okay. They're well done but they're fine.

BEN You know, I think I need to go to the emergency room.

KENNY Really?

BEN Yeah, I mean it's not stopping.

MARY Paul Bunyan! We can meet Paul Bunyan!

BEN I think *you* need to take me to the emergency room.

KENNY Okay.

BEN I'll send Mary inside.

KENNY She can stay here.

BEN No no no no no no. She's drunk.

MARY I'm not drunk! I'm planning a trip.

BEN She needs to go home.

SHARON Kenny, help. Kenny, help, it's happening—

KENNY It's not happening.

SHARON Just like they said it would happen in our meetings—

KENNY Sharon—

SHARON They said our old life would feel like real life and our new life would feel like a dream. I'm dreaming right now.

BEN No you're not.

SHARON (*starting to hyperventilate*) I am. I can feel it. I'm
    dreaming—

MARY *grabs* SHARON *in some awkward and intimate way.* BEN
and KENNY *are trying to deal with* BEN's *cut leg.*

MARY No you're not. You're here, Sharon. I am here. And
    we are going camping. For real. This is not a dream.

Blackout.

SCENE 5

Night sounds.

The lights rise and SHARON *is tiptoeing onto* MARY*'s back porch wearing a T-shirt and underwear. Maybe a ratty robe? Suddenly* MARY *opens the sliding door. She is dressed in pajamas. They look at each other for a moment.*

MARY Too excited to sleep?

SHARON Yes!

MARY Oh my god, me too! I can't believe we're actually going! Do you know the campground is only twelve miles away from here? I've googled it so many times. In case of emergency. I sit there and look at the website and imagine.

SHARON I got hot dogs and buns and coffee.

MARY I got bug spray and bacon and toast.

SHARON We can make bacon?

MARY I'm bringing a frying pan!

Do they giggle like little girls?

SHARON I think nature is really going to help. Mary, every day really is a new day. But Mary, I open my eyes every morning and all I want is a pipe to smoke. It's like there's a fire burning in the center of my head, Mary, and the pipe is the water that will put it out. And I say this at our meetings, and they are all very supportive, but the fire only goes down a little bit. Every day, all day. And in the middle of this burning I am supposed to envision my life, Mary. I'm supposed to set goals and maybe take night classes that will expand my horizons. And I guess that works, Mary, I guess so. But to be honest, I feel like the real opportunities are the ones that fall into your lap. Like winning the lottery or someone's rich uncle needing a personal assistant. That almost happened to me once, Mary. And everything would have been different.

Mary, I fell off the wagon for a day. I called in sick and walked down to the gas station and bought a stash from the kid with the skateboard. And I got high right there, Mary, in the parking lot by the Dumpster. And I walked home, and nobody fucking walks here, so I stuck out like a sore thumb, and I got lost a little, so I wound up walking around the neighborhood—which looks soooooooo beautiful when you're high, especially when you let the street signs really sink in—and this guy in a pickup truck gave me a ride home—by that time I had accidentally walked out of one of my shoes and didn't realize it, Mary. So anyway we were talking in his truck outside my house and he finally said, "Are you high?" and I said, "Yes, I am" and he told me about all the ways he parties. He does ecstasy, he eats mushrooms, and every now and then but not too often he shoots heroin. But he's careful because he doesn't want to get hooked on it. Oh, and sometimes he takes ludes and sometimes he does whip-its just to remind himself of high school. All like three streets away from here, on Solar Power Lane. And I said, "What do you do for a living?" And he said, "I'm an electrician. I do house calls." And I said, "How do you afford all that stash?" And he wouldn't tell me. And I said "Do you want to be an electrician forever?" And he said what he really wanted to do was be a marine biologist, and we were just getting into this amazing conversation about the many varieties of sharks—the guy was rubbing my feet—when Kenny came home.

Kenny knew immediately what I had done.

He was nice to the guy, considering.

I spent the rest of the day drinking Diet Coke and watching Jerry Springer and then like four hours screaming my face off and trying to escape. Somehow Kenny tied me to the wall, to the door handles.

MARY What?

SHARON No, no he had to. He had to.

MARY This all happened—

SHARON Two days ago. Between the last time I saw you and now.

MARY Jesus.

SHARON I know.

MARY I think I was at work pretending to type a letter while surfing the Internet looking for plastic outdoor tablecloths.

SHARON This is a nice table. You don't need a tablecloth.

MARY I know. I just get bored with it every now and then. (SHARON *notices the light on. She looks at it*) He's working on his website. (*they both look for a second more*) And Kenny's still letting you go?

SHARON Kenny thinks you're good for me.

MARY Aw. (*she is a little touched by that*)

SHARON And what about your life? Do you feel like a construction worker building a house, or a twig floating in the stream?

MARY (*laughs*) You say some funny things sometimes.

SHARON Washing our faces in the fresh water. Gathering a few nuts.

MARY Sharon.

SHARON Yup.

MARY Why don't you have any furniture in your house?

SHARON Because we're broke. Crazy broke. I mean I'm thirty-four years old and I still eat ramen noodles for dinner a lot. Because we have to.

MARY What's going to happen to you?

SHARON What do you mean?

MARY I just . . . I don't understand . . . how you and Kenny . . . are ever . . . I mean something's going to happen again . . . and you're going to be . . . I mean, how many times do you get to . . .

SHARON You've got to live this moment, Mary. That's all you can do. I'm as beautiful on the inside as you are. (*she touches* MARY'*s face*)

The sliding glass door opens. BEN *comes out. He is wearing a cast on one leg. He's not alarmed, just curious.*

BEN What's going on?

MARY We're too excited to sleep!

BEN You girls are going to get eaten by bears!

SHARON Stop it! I hate bears.

MARY There's no *bears* around here. Sheesh.

BEN Come get some sleep.

MARY Good night, Sharon.

SHARON *mumbles good night.* MARY *and* BEN *go inside.* SHARON *scratches each of her arms. She goes toward her backyard.*

Blackout.

SCENE 6

What are the sounds? Is it the neighborhood sounds, only processed?
Or is it construction sounds because they are knocking down the
house a few blocks over?

    The lights come up. KENNY *and* BEN *are sitting on the front*
steps of BEN'*s house.* BEN *has a light cast on his ankle and shin. It*
is afternoon. They are each drinking a beer, like a Budweiser. They
are quiet for a couple of seconds.

KENNY Well, whatever new job I get they're gonna garnish
    the paychecks.

BEN Have you ever thought of sitting down with a credit
    specialist?

KENNY I thought I *was* sitting down with a credit specialist.

BEN And how much do those specialists usually cost? When
    you pay full price? (*silence for a moment*) I'm not asking
    for a lot of money. I just need to place some value on
    my time. Services cost money. If you offer something
    for free, it is seen as having less value. My book told
    me this.

KENNY How is twenty-five dollars going to make a differ-
    ence to you right now?

BEN It's the principle. I've got to stick by my principles. (*they both take a sip of beer*) It's not a lot of money.

KENNY Let's see, we'll see. I've got a court case I'm waiting on in Arkansas. It's gonna save us, if it comes through.

BEN In Arkansas?

KENNY I slipped and fell in a supermarket a few years ago. That's how I hurt my back. That's why I have to wear the weight-lifting belt. The belt that cost me my job.

BEN Right.

KENNY When I get that settlement, I'll give you your twenty-five dollars and you can give me more "advice."

BEN All right. (*a few seconds*) Are you supposed to be drinking that?

KENNY One is okay.

They sip.

KENNY So are you ready to start taking "real" clients?

BEN I better. I have one more month of severance pay.

KENNY One more month and you'll be just like me.

BEN I guess so, yeah.

KENNY Bruh-thaaaz. (BEN *and* KENNY *clink beer cans*)

KENNY How much you want to bet they're gonna call us any minute. Ah! There's snakes! There's roaches!

BEN I don't know that their cell phones work out there.

KENNY "Come out here! It's dark!" And you know what, we're not gonna go.

BEN Well—

KENNY No really, they're out there in nature, sitting in the menstrual hut, eating crickets, whatever, that's what they want, and we have to honor that. We have to let the women be women.

BEN They better not come back wanting to burn that . . . that . . .

KENNY Sage stick.

BEN Yeah! I went to a wedding once where they did that. So weird.

KENNY That stuff stinks.

BEN Wearing feathers and a deerskin skirt. (*they both laugh*)

KENNY So whaddaya say, brothah? Boys' night out. There's Dan's Place and Déjà Vu and Temptations and Barely Legal.

BEN I don't know—really?

KENNY I've only been to Dan's Place and Déjà Vu. Déjà Vu is upscale, but Dan's Place is traaa-shee!

BEN I mean really, I should work.

KENNY Work? It's Saturday. Our wives are away—

BEN I know, but maybe—

KENNY We're just embracing our human nature, man—

BEN But Kenny, those clubs are expensive.

KENNY We're just relaxing after a hard week's work.

BEN The drinks alone are like nine bucks. And it's usually a three-drink minimum. It adds up, and then what?

KENNY Aw, man. Aw, man is that what this is about? You think it's irresponsible? For us to have a night out? For *me* to have a night out?

BEN No, I didn't say that. It's just . . . it's just one night . . . if we take a step back for a second—

KENNY Oh god, that fucking book!

BEN I have . . . I have a vision for my life, Kenny.

KENNY So do I, douche bag.

BEN Hey, hey, hey. This is coming out wrong. I mean I don't even know how . . . can we . . . can we just drink, please?

KENNY Hmph. (*both men take a sip*) You're a good man, Ben.

BEN I don't know.

KENNY No really, you are.

BEN In a parallel universe I'm a good man.

KENNY I'm an asshole.

BEN No you're not.

KENNY I'm like, "You too good for yellow mustard!?" right in the middle of the store.

BEN You're under a lot of stress.

KENNY I'm an *asshole*, and it's too late for me.

BEN *doesn't know what to say. The two men sip their beers.*

BEN I think this might be against the law.

KENNY What?

BEN Drinking beers in the front yard.

KENNY You own your house, right?

BEN Of course. Well, I mean the bank owns it—

KENNY Shit then, private property. You gotta hang on to that house, Ben.

BEN Of course.

KENNY Don't let anyone take it from you.

BEN No, no, we're fine. I mean we haven't even dipped into our savings and I don't think we'll have to. We're not . . . we're not anywhere near that yet.

KENNY Hang on to that house. That's what my grandfather
     always used to say to my dad.
BEN And did he hang on to it?

KENNY *doesn't say anything. It is obvious his dad did NOT hang
on to the house.*
    *Silence. Sound of the suburbs. Kids in the distance on bikes. A
plane overhead. The compressors for several central air-conditioning
units. Hovering a little closer than usual, pressing in.*
    BEN *contemplates boys' night out.*

BEN I mean I've got this leg.
KENNY I bet it could get you a sympathy lap dance.
BEN I don't know.
KENNY I'll drive.
BEN It's just such a hassle to *go* anywhere.
KENNY We deserve it, Ben.

*A few moments of silence, where they sit and watch and sip. Then
BEN finishes his beer and crushes his can.*

BEN All right, let's do it.
KENNY Serious!
BEN Yeah, you decide where we're going and you have to
     drive. Except I've been to Dan's too, and it really is
     too skankified, so not there.
KENNY You've been?
BEN Sure for an um bachelor party.
KENNY Yeah right.
BEN So maybe one rung up the ladder. (*he looks down the street*)

KENNY Temptations, then. Let's try Temptations.

BEN Should we get dinner first?

KENNY Nah, man, let's just eat something here.

BEN We've got nothing in the house.

KENNY Fuck it, let's scrounge. I've got a can of Manwich.

BEN I think we have hot dogs.

KENNY Yeah, we'll chop 'em up, mix 'em around.

BEN Spaghetti? Over spaghetti?

KENNY Oh man, no. I think maybe no—

BEN All right, we might have some white bread.

KENNY My brothah, we're good to go! Chow down and get there in time for happy hour.

BEN I think it's two for one navel shots.

Kenny kind of dances and sings that line from the song "Hey Ya" by Outkast.

KENNY Awright, awright, awright—

BEN That's what they advertise, anyway.

KENNY (*this next speech cracks* BEN *up*) See! For two brothahs on a budget! For two MEN whose wives are out playing survivor. For two men in need of a little R and R after a tough couple of weeks. For two men in search of a little good, clean fun. For two men in need of a boys' night out. For two men who appreciate God's gift to this green earth. Who appreciate that special titty talent of the special titty dancer. For two men who want to feel more connected to their bodies and to the world. Who want to get out of the house and live a little. For two men who aren't afraid to have a good time even though their financial lives are swirling around in some kind of homemade toilet bowl—

BEN Come on—

KENNY For two men who are men. For two men who are going to have a great fucking night. For two men who are going to have a fucking great fucking night on the town, not far from their house. For two men who can take one night to not worry so much, to go out on the town and engage with the nightlife, with the life of the night, who want to see what kind of good, clean fun is out there and if in the process they get their hands a little dirty, well, hey, it was in the name of good, clean fun. For two men who, oh shit . . . oh shit . . . oh shit . . . oh shit . . . (KENNY *sees something down the street.* BEN *looks*)

BEN Oh shit.

KENNY Oh shit.

BEN *takes the beer cans and tosses them behind the bushes.*

KENNY Oh shit. Shit.

SHARON *and* MARY *walk up. They carry pretty big backpacks, like camping backpacks, on their backs.*

MARY Hi!

SHARON Hello! We didn't make it!

MARY We didn't make it!

BEN I guess not.

71

BEN *hops up, hopping on one foot, and helps* MARY *take her back-pack off.*

MARY First we drove out onto the loop and got totally lost.

SHARON We thought we were going *toward* the campground, but actually we were going away.

MARY And then all of a sudden we were in this tiny town called Sooter.

BEN Oh, that's where the minor-league baseball field is.

SHARON And there was this store with a little lunch counter.

MARY Can you believe it? It was like straight out of an old history book.

SHARON And so we had sandwiches and Diet Cokes.

MARY And the guy gave us directions *back* to the campground. And I went to pee and we got back on the road.

SHARON And we were on our way and then *I* had to pee.

MARY So we got off the interstate and stopped at a gas station.

SHARON And I peed in this nas-tee bathroom while Mary flirted with the counter guy—

MARY I did not! I bought a pack of Big Red.

SHARON "Big Red"

MARY Shut up!

SHARON And then we were pulling out of the gas station and the car started making this crazy-ass noise.

MARY Like the gears were crunching together.

SHARON Like the car was eating celery mixed with ice cubes.

MARY So we stopped the car and the guy from the gas station came to look at it and he fooled around for like thirty minutes and did something with the gears—

SHARON He rigged it with a coat hanger!

MARY And we asked if he thought it was okay for us to take the car to the campground. And he said sure it should, the campground is close. So we got in the car and we set off, but we were really quiet.

SHARON For like ten minutes we didn't talk. And finally Mary said, "Sharon, are you afraid of breaking down in the woods?"

MARY (*pointing to* SHARON) And she said, "*Yes!* I'm terrified! I never thought about breaking down before we left!"

SHARON There are bears in the woods!

BEN There aren't really bears.

MARY And I started thinking about my foot. And how I didn't have a clean bandage. And the wet ground.

SHARON Slugs. Dead Frogs.

MARY And I said, "Well, it's late, so maybe we should just—"

MARY and SHARON Go home—

MARY And right that second I saw the exit for Richfield Road, the back way home, and so I cut across three lanes of traffic.

SHARON I spilled my Diet Coke all over the window!

MARY And I started laughing so hard I almost peed myself, even though I had just peed!

SHARON And we started laughing so hard we kind of swerved to the side of the road. And BAM!

MARY A flat tire! So I pulled over—I mean I've changed a flat tire before—

BEN And you didn't have a spare.

MARY I didn't have a spare!

BEN I haven't had a chance to get a new one since we popped the old one.

MARY And we canceled triple A to save money, so we were like, well, do we call the guys or maybe a gas station and *wait* for them to come here? Or do we *hike* the twenty minutes home?

SHARON A hike. That's like camping.

MARY Sure it is!

SHARON So that's what we did!

MARY We fucking hiked!!

BEN (*quick, re: her cursing*) Mary—

SHARON And here we are! I hate camping anyway. All those *bugs*!

MARY And rapists!

SHARON Baby, did you miss me?

MARY We got catcalled.

SHARON We thought maybe we could party here.

MARY We thought maybe we'd grill.

BEN We've got to get the car, I guess.

KENNY I've got a spare you can use.

BEN Thanks, Kenny.

KENNY Just a fifteen-dollar charge. For the rental. (*quick moment of quiet*) Just kidding!

BEN All right, let's go.

MARY We'll get together some snacks.

SHARON It's so weird how nothing ever happens.

KENNY I'll get my keys.

KENNY *leaves and goes into his house.*

BEN We were going to watch soccer.

SHARON You keep thinking things are going to happen, but nothing ever does.

MARY You don't watch soccer.

BEN Kenny likes soccer. He lived in Ireland for a year when he was a kid.

SHARON No he didn't.

BEN What?

SHARON Jesus, that stupid story.

MARY It's funny, just making the *effort* to go camping made me feel a lot better.

KENNY *comes back with his keys.*

BEN All right, well, should we grill?

SHARON "Almost" only counts in horseshoes and hand grenades.

MARY (*a little over the top, a little dorky*) It's Saturday night! Let's have a goooooooooood time.

Quick moment where BEN, SHARON, *and* KENNY *are like "Huh? That was sort of dorky."* MARY *doesn't notice.*

Blackout.

SCENE 7

Night sounds. Then the sound of music, low. Some kind of party music. Maybe music from SHARON *and* KENNY'S *Hotlanta days? It gets louder and louder. When the lights come up,* BEN, KENNY, *and* MARY *are dancing their asses off on* BEN *and* MARY'S *porch.* BEN *is dancing on a chair with his broken leg.* KENNY *is fake humping the grill.* MARY *is spinning in circles. They are all beer wasted. Which is different from bourbon wasted. Bourbon makes you mean and switches on your regret.*

BEN Yay-eah, yay-eah, yay-eah yay-eah yay-eah.

MARY I'm a sexy mothafuckah on yo roof.

    I'm a sexy mothafuckah on yo back porch

    I'm a sexy mothafuckah in yo kitchen

    I'm a sexy mothafuckah on yo lawn.

KENNY (*wailing, high-pitched R & B style*) I'm your lover I'm your daddy I'm your car tire I'm your devil I'm your sexy

    I'm your burger I'm your boyfriend

    I'm your superstar!

BEN (*singing at the same time as* KENNY) Yay-eah, yay-eah, yay-eah yay-eah yay-eah.

BEN (*wailing too, after* KENNY *has finished*) I'm your superstar!
   I'm your superstar!
MARY Hey Ben, do this! Do this! Ben, do this!

MARY *does some kind of dance move she wants* BEN *to do.* BEN *does it.* KENNY *comes up behind* MARY *and dirty dances with her a little.*

MARY Wait! Everybody do this! Do it! (*She does a dance move. They don't do it*) DO IT! (*the two guys do it, they are all in a line*) We're on that show! You know that show with the dancers.
BEN Yay-eah, yay-eah, yay-eah yay-eah yay-eah.
KENNY I was on that show when I was sixteen!
MARY Really!
KENNY No. Sometimes I just say shit.
BEN Look, I'm doing the one-legged twist.

KENNY *cracks up.* MARY *twists with* BEN. KENNY *cracks up more.*

KENNY That is some funny shit.

KENNY *starts doing some weird, vaguely John Travolta-esque humping of the air, almost like he is swinging his dick around. Or maybe using barbecue tongs as his dick?*

MARY Kenny!
BEN (*kind of cracking up but kind of like "what?"*) Holy shit!
KENNY (*wails and grinds*) I'm a superstar!
MARY and BEN I'm a superstar.

SHARON *enters with two bowls—one filled with water and one filled with some other kind of food. She puts them on the floor and looks at them.*

KENNY What are you doing?

SHARON I'm feeding my dog. I have a dog, remember? I'm feeding it.

KENNY Oh that is fucking funny. (*he gets two beers out of the cooler*)

MARY Oh right, your dog! You love your dog!

BEN Ha-ha, that is fucking funny.

SHARON Now I'm walking my dog.

SHARON *fake-walks her dog. It is on a leash and she kind of dances while she does it. The others crack up.*

KENNY Walk that dog.

SHARON *walks the dog sexier. The others take up fake leashes and walk their dogs, dancing while they do so.*

MARY Oh no, my dog just pooped! Look at me!

She pretends to pick up the dog shit with a fake bag and throws the bag away. They all hoot and holler and cheer while she does so. SHARON *steps up onto the table and walks her dog up there.* KENNY *hands her a beer and she gulps it down.*

MARY Are you allowed to have that?

SHARON (*keeps dancing*) Yeah sure, it's just beer.

KENNY Her problem was really freebasing heroin, anyway.

SHARON Kenny!

MARY That was a joke, right?

BEN Yay-eah, yay-eah, yay-eah yay-eah yay-eah.

SHARON Yay-eah, yay-eah, yay-eah yay-eah yay-eah.

KENNY *gets up on the table and starts dancing with* SHARON. BEN *and* MARY *walk their dogs.*

MARY Oh my god I just got the greatest idea.

SHARON What?

MARY We should all fake-walk our dogs over to the lady in the pink jogging suit's house! We should fake-walk our dogs over there and have them take a fake crap on their lawn! And we'll be like whoooooo hoooooo!

BEN Let's do it!

SHARON Oh my god, that's hilarious.

MARY, BEN, *and* SHARON *start to go.* KENNY *starts herding them back: he is a seasoned partier and he knows that crazy shit could bring cops and spoil everything.*

KENNY No no no, we're going to stay back here.

MARY Come on!

KENNY Come on, let's keep the party here. No no, come on.

MARY Party pooper!

SHARON (*cracks up*) Get it? Party pooper!

MARY *cracks up.* MARY *and* SHARON *fake poop or fake fart on* KENNY.

KENNY All right, bitches!

KENNY *picks both ladies up and spins them around. The la-*
dies squeal. He puts them down and the three of them dirty dance
for a few seconds. BEN *sits on the patio table with his feet on a*
chair.

SHARON Come on, Ben!
BEN Just a second, I'm resting.
MARY No! No resting! No resting! No resting resting resting
      resting!

It becomes a chant. BEN *kind of dances in his seat.* MARY *couple*
dances with SHARON.

MARY Oh my god, I really needed this! Some downtime!
BEN It feels good just to release!

The patio table breaks, and BEN *falls to the ground. A moment,*
they look, just music; then BEN *jumps up.*

BEN I'm okay!

They all chant and dance, and maybe do a little "He's okay!"
chant. BEN *dances with everyone.* SHARON *acts like she is holding*
a giant cup.

SHARON Guess what this is? (*everybody says "What?"*)
SHARON It's a giant cup of party juice, and I'm drinking it
      down!

Everyone hoots and hollers as SHARON *drinks.* MARY *pretends to*
be holding something over her head.

MARY Guess what this is? (*everybody says "What?"*)

MARY It's a big bowl of get-down and I'm pouring it all over you!

They all hoot, holler, and get down as MARY *pours the fake juice.* KENNY *pretends to be holding something over his arm, like a purse.*

KENNY Guess what this is? (*everybody says "What?"*)

KENNY It's my handbasket and we're all going to hell in it!

Everybody hoots and hollers "Going to hell! Going to hell!" SHARON *starts dirty dancing with* BEN. *Pretty quickly they start to make out. Pretty quickly it is pretty hot.* MARY *and* KENNY *are still dancing and saying "Going to hell!" Then* MARY *sees* SHARON *and* BEN *and stops dead in her tracks. She reaches out for* KENNY's *arm. He is still dancing.*

MARY Kenny, what's happening? What is that?

KENNY Oh, it's nothing, nothing. Hold on.

KENNY *dances over and dances* SHARON *away from* BEN. *He dances with* SHARON *and whispers in her ear.* SHARON *kind of giggles and says "You're right, you're right" only to* KENNY. BEN *is shell-shocked for a minute and then starts dancing again.* MARY *is shell-shocked for a minute longer and starts dancing again.* KENNY *is dancing with* SHARON, *and when* MARY *isn't looking,* SHARON *looks to* BEN *and mouths the words "Sorry, I'm sorry" to him.* BEN *smiles at her and kind of shrugs his shoulders and laughs back.*

KENNY *and* SHARON *start making out.* BEN *and* MARY *get a little uncomfortable and sort of half dance.* KENNY *grabs* SHARON's *ass in this major way, like his finger is sliding down the back of her*

ass crack on top of her pants over and down between her legs.
SHARON *kind of rides his leg.* MARY *freaks a little.*

MARY Okay okay okay okay! I think we are stopping! I think
it is time for us to be stopping!
SHARON (*breaks away from* KENNY) No, no, no, no stopping!
No stopping!
MARY Weird things are happening!
SHARON No, no. *Things* are happening. Can't you see?
BEN It's okay, Mary, don't worry.
MARY I'm going to call the police.
KENNY No you're not.
MARY I mean somebody—somebody is going to call the
police.
BEN It's our house. We're on our lawn.
SHARON This is nothing compared to what's going down on
Solar Power Lane right now.
MARY Yes, but they do it quietly.
SHARON (*yelling*) AND WE DO IT LOUD! Whoooo!
KENNY (*turns the music up a bit*) Just keep dancing, Mary, it gets
the endorphins going. We learned this in rehab. It can
take the place of drugs. But you have to keep moving.

MARY *keeps moving: half dancing, half exercising.*

SHARON It's beautiful! You're beautiful, Mary.

SHARON *kisses* MARY *deeply.* MARY *lets her. The guys watch.*
SHARON *lets go.*

MARY Did that really happen?

SHARON Of course it did! Things can happen. You can just *do* them. You have to just *do* them. If you don't, then the world just stays the same.

Music. Music. MARY *busts a chair on the cement patio. Music. Music. Is* BEN *going to be mad?*

BEN Whooooooo—hoooooo!

Another mad round of dancing. On chairs, with each other. Nothing really sexual, just mad dancing. At some point BEN *breaks another chair.*

BEN I hate these fucking chairs! Who wants a chair that you can break with one hand?
MARY They were on clearance from Patio Depot.
BEN Fuck Patio Depot!

They cheer and dance. SHARON *starts piling up the wood from the chairs.* KENNY *downs another beer.* MARY *starts a chant.*

MARY I'm feeling, I'm feeling, I'm feeling, I'm feeling . . .
    (KENNY *joins her*)
KENNY and MARY I'm feeling I'm feeling I'm feeling I'm feeling.
KENNY Take it, Mary!
MARY I'm feeling electricity, electricity running through my arms and legs—
KENNY Yeah!
MARY It's in my blood, the electricity is in my blood!

SHARON That's good!

KENNY I'm feeling, I'm feeling, I'm feeling—

MARY Yes, Kenny?

KENNY I'm feeling like my whole body is filled up with some kind of sweet air, strawberry air, and strawberry shortcake air—

MARY Whooo!

KENNY And it's making me feel like I can do fucking anything!

MARY Waaaaaahhhhh!

KENNY Look at me!

BEN I'm feeling, I'm feeling . . . (KENNY *joins him*)

KENNY and BEN I'm feeling, I'm feeling, I'm feeling . . .

BEN I'm feeling like telling the truth!

KENNY Yeah!

MARY Tell it! Tell it! Tell it tell it tell it!

SHARON *breaks another chair and keeps piling wood.*

BEN Should I?

MARY Tell it baby tell it!

MARY and KENNY Tell it baby tell it!

SHARON We're here for you! We'll catch you! It's a truth fall, a trust fall!

Does SHARON *get* BEN *to stand on a chair?*

BEN I'm feeling it!

MARY Say it!

BEN (*still in party chant mode*) All right!

I have no website! I said there ain't no website!

I have no website, I have no business cards, I have no plan, I got nothing! Nothing nothing nothing!

KENNY Yea-ah, yeah-ah, yeah-ah yeah-ah yeah-ah!

MARY What?

KENNY *is dancing around.*

BEN After seven whole weeks.

I've got nothing!

Nothing to show!

Nothing to show show show!

MARY What, did your computer crash or something?

BEN No. I just. I think I don't want to, Mary.

MARY You don't want to?

BEN I mean I've got a domain name. A domain name that I own. On the Internet. But I don't think I want to run a financial planning business.

MARY Well, what do you want to do?

KENNY Ben's got nothing! Ben's got nothing!

SHARON *joins in.* MARY *and* BEN *are still, looking at each other.*

KENNY and SHARON Ben's got nothing! Ben's got nothing! Ben's got nothing!

MARY No!

SHARON and KENNY Ben's got nothing!

MARY NOOO!

MARY *kind of runs at* BEN, *to hit him.* SHARON *and* KENNY *catch her.*

SHARON No no no, Mary. It's a beautiful thing, Mary! Do you know what just happened? Do you realize what just happened? A beautiful thing has happened!

Ben just admitted he's at zero.

And guess what, Mary?

When you are at zero, anything can happen.

It's like total possibility.

BEN Yeah, Mary.

SHARON He's like a tennis player with his knees bent, poised to jump in any direction.

It's a beautiful thing, Mary.

BEN Yeah, Mary.

MARY But what are we going to do?

A moment. Then SHARON.

SHARON We are going to start a fire.

BEN Huh?

KENNY Really?

SHARON Yeah, just like we used to do in Plano.

KENNY Yeah, but that was Texas.

SHARON Yes, but it's such a beautiful thing.

KENNY True dat.

SHARON It's a ritual, a healing ritual for Mary and Ben. Their clearance patio furniture will go up into the air, like a flower petal on the wind. And then you will be at zero, together.

MARY Um.

SHARON *couple dances with* MARY.

SHARON We're going to do this, Mary. It's going to happen right here before your eyes. And it is going to open up a space.

MARY What kind of space?

SHARON You are living inside a tiny spectrum, Mary. (*she shows* MARY *with her fingers—pinching her forefinger to her thumb*) Like this small. And do you know how big the spectrum really is, Mary? Do you know?

MARY I don't know.

SHARON Light it, Kenny.

KENNY *lights a match. Somehow, the pile of wood instantly catches fire. A roaring fire. They are all mesmerized.*

MARY A campfire!

BEN Whoa. Isn't that kind of big?

MARY You're taking me camping!

SHARON Yes, Mary. Yes.

KENNY *dances around the fire a bit.*

MARY I can feel the heat. And the wind. Going into my eyes. I can feel my eyeballs and my inner ear, my inner ears. And I feel a splitting feeling, like maybe in my bones down here, the bones that make up my hips. I feel a splitting feeling, Ben. Ben? Where are you? (*she goes to* BEN)

BEN The funny thing is, I always wanted to be British, but I never really told anyone.

MARY My forehead separating from my skull.

BEN When I was ten, I would watch *Masterpiece Theater*

and read Agatha Christie, and when I would go to McDonald's I would order iced tea because I thought that is what a British person would do.

And there was a whole year, when I was eight, when I ate all my sandwiches with the crusts off. Until one time I got beat up for doing that and so I stopped.

I think I've felt British from the moment I first opened my eyes.

SHARON *goes to* BEN *and* MARY. *At some point, both couples stand together before the fire, in a kind of group hug. This is a shared experience.*

MARY I think I am feeling another skin just below my real skin. It's been there the whole time.

BEN I rolled up my pants just above my ankle for a time. "For a time." That sounds kind of British. Falling asleep wondering what a crumpet was.

SHARON That's so sweet. Mary, are you hearing this?

MARY Yes.

BEN And the funny thing is, Mary, there is a website out there called Brit-Land, and it is designed especially for non-Brits who want to be British. And I have an identity on that website. A British identity. It all plays out in real time.

SHARON and KENNY Tell us, tell us . . .

BEN My name is Ian. I'm a prep school teacher. I teach history. I like to bike. I have a cat. I am engaged to be married. I drink a pint of ale each afternoon.

Right now I am asleep because I like to get up

early to go for my jog and a cuppa tea before heading to campus.

Right now I am asleep in my flat.

The fire is getting pretty big.

MARY Huh?

BEN Right now I am asleep in my flat. With my girlfriend Julia. I spend more time there than I do on my website, Mary. I spend quite a bit of time in Brit-Land.

SHARON That's amazing!

KENNY Anybody got marshmallows?

SHARON So much is happening right now!

MARY Yes, but is the table supposed to be on fire too? Is that really happening?

They look into the kitchen.

KENNY Uh . . .

BEN Oh shit. Look at the curtains!

MARY Somebody call the . . . oh shit. My phone is inside.

SHARON This could be good! This could be amazing!

SHARON and KENNY dance.

MARY Ben, let's go next door. Quick, let's go next door!

MARY helps BEN off the porch. SHARON and KENNY keep dancing as the lights

Blackout.

SCENE 8

We hear the sound of fire burning, of the fire getting bigger. We hear neighbors and sirens and the crackling of wood. We hear the shouting of firemen. We hear the whoosh of water coming out of the fire hoses.

We hear the fire die down. We hear the neighbors start to disperse. We hear the police arrive and ask questions. We hear the wet wood smoldering. We hear the last cinder popping. We hear the fire trucks drive away. We hear the morning breaking. We hear no more voices. We hear morning sounds, pretty much like any other early morning in the Bright Houses subdivision.

The lights come up on MARY *and* BEN *standing in front of their burned-down house.* SHARON *and* KENNY*'s house stands next to theirs. Their front door is wide open.*

There is a man standing with them. He's dressed casually, like in a plaid shirt and blue pants. The style of his clothes is just a little out of date.

This is KENNY*'s great-uncle. The keeper of the house* SHARON *and* KENNY *were living in. His name is* FRANK.

FRANK I lived around the corner for twenty-nine years.
      Bought one of the model homes, the houses people
      would come pick from. There were five of them, and
      every house in the neighborhood was one of the five.

Hard to tell now, because people have redone things, repainted, knocked down, rebuilt. But yes, there were five model homes and you just picked the one you liked and they built it for you. You could choose some colors, and you could decide things like if you wanted the closet here or there, but mostly they just built it from the model. It was no big deal that your house looked like a lot of the other houses. It was a new house! You were living in Bright Houses. It was like stealing second base. You were safe.

They were magic times. Kids running ragged everywhere, skinning their knees, catching beetles. Lemonade stands. All the fathers pulling into the driveways at five-thirty sharp in their Belvederes, their Furies. Kids running up into their arms. Our arms.

And two Saturdays a month in the summertime were the Noontime at Night dances. They'd light up the pavilion with all these colored lights and you'd dance till you had blisters on your blisters. Everybody's shoes tossed off to the side. All outdoors! Nobody had any money. We all doubled up on babysitters. We'd pick up little Walter and Katie from the floor of Ed and Shirley's house at two or three in the morning sometimes.

I mean, not everyone was living this life. It was 1968. But the whole country wasn't hippies. Most of us were just living like this. (*he looks at* KENNY *and* SHARON*'s house*)

Roger was my niece Donna's son. I never got to know him all that well. Donna never quite settled down—Roger was her son with her first husband,

and then she had two girls with the man I think she's still with now. I don't think they married.

I knew Roger best when he was nine years old. We would have them over for Thanksgiving. I took him fishing for perch a couple times—there used to be a pond, you know, at the end of Feather Way, where they keep the bulldozers now.

He was a good kid.

I heard about his trouble in high school. At first the arrests sounded like typical boy stuff—graffiti, cheap wine. Even when his son was born, when Roger was seventeen, it seemed like it was going to be okay. He was working for a construction company. His girlfriend, the mother of his child, cleaned houses. Sometimes those things work. Sometimes a child focuses you toward your life.

BEN We didn't know he had a son.

FRANK Well, to be honest, I stopped keeping track the last five, ten years. He was my great-nephew, and I wasn't even that close with his mother, my niece Donna. She moved to Nebraska years ago and seemed to want to . . . separate herself from us. She's a high school guidance counselor.

But I know Roger's had troubles. Drugs. And I think a spell in jail. Spells in jail. And when Roger came to me with this new girl all dressed up to ask about staying in the house, I told him I'd think about it and give him a call.

And I never gave him a call. It was a can of worms I thought best to keep closed.

They got in through a back window, I guess. I bet he fixed it right away. Roger always was a handy guy. Got in through the back window and then probably never locked the door.

MARY They really didn't have much of anything in the house.

FRANK It's spooky in there. There's just a mattress and a coffee table and some dirty laundry. A few dishes. Sheetrock's all banged up in the bedroom. I think there's blood too.

MARY He went by Kenny. He told us his name was Kenny.

FRANK Kenny, huh? No, it's Roger. It's always been Roger.

Well, I'm going to put padlocks on the front and back doors and the big windows. I'll be back in the next few days to clean the place out. I don't think they'll come back, but if they do, I can't let them in. They've done enough already.

BEN They weren't bad people. They were trying.

FRANK Mm-hmm.

MARY We enjoyed them.

FRANK Ma'am, they burned your house down.

The sounds of Bright Houses: cars, the hum of air compressors, kids in the distance, etc.

FRANK To be honest it hurts my heart to come back here. Half the houses falling apart, the others so fancified they seem untouchable. (*he indicates a large house across the street*) I mean, how are you going to ask for a cup of sugar from someone who lives in *that* place? You'd have to buy a new pair of shoes just to walk up their driveway. This is not what the developers intended. They wanted you to have neighbors. They wanted you to be in it together.

Do you two have some help?

BEN What?

FRANK Help. Family, friends? To help you clean up, rebuild?

BEN Oh yeah, we have insurance. For this sort of thing.

FRANK Insurance isn't going to bring by a home-cooked casserole.

MARY Well, we're in a hotel tonight.

BEN Our parents might come. And I have a brother.

FRANK Well, I wish you the best. I really do. And, well, here. (*He takes a couple of bills out of his wallet.* BEN *and* MARY *are like "no . . . no"*) No, really. I would like to give you a little something. I feel like I participated in this somehow. I'd like to help. (BEN *takes the money*)

You know, someone should really start an archive about this place and the things that happened here. I'm going to get my granddaughter to help me go on the Internet and help me find people who lived here over the years. My granddaughter—whoo! She can find anything on the Web. She helped me get driving directions from Dublin to Galway in *Ireland*. Like that! (*he snaps his fingers*) She could help me, I bet. Find people and ask them for photos. It's easy now to get copies made at the machine in the drugstore, and they could mail them to me parcel post and I could put them all into one big book. Maybe with memories written out next to each one.

I think my sister Lois had a picture of herself standing right there, planting that tree, come to think of it . . . That could kick off the album . . . And we could put the book here somewhere . . . maybe where the old pavilion was, and folks could come look through it, to see what life used to be like. I'm going to follow up on that idea with my granddaughter. An archive. (*sounds again*)

All right, then. Well, it's very nice getting to know you.

Oh, and some lady came by asking about a dog? Roger's dog? She seems very concerned to know that Roger had taken his dog with him.

MARY I'm sure he did.

FRANK She insisted that I check. If you see it, let me know. Okay then. Nice to know you. Heck, we're practically neighbors, just a decade or two apart. I do hope you'll rebuild.

BEN *and* MARY *smile.*

MARY We're thinking of moving to Britain.

FRANK Oh. Really?

MARY Ian's got some family over there. I'd like to have a farm.

FRANK Oh well, Britain's great. Beautiful place. Nice people.

MARY Not really. I find them a bit snooty.

BEN (*in a British accent*) A bit snooty, yes.

FRANK Oh, well, then, I don't really know about that.

Well, we'll miss ya. The neighborhood will miss ya, that is. So long now.

MARY So long.

FRANK *signs off, walks to his car.* MARY *and* BEN *are alone in front of their house.* BEN *pulls some forms out of his back pocket.*

MARY What's that?

BEN They want a list of things that didn't burn.

MARY That didn't burn?

BEN Something about our net worth (*He looks at the form. Then he looks at* MARY) You know my website isn't as bad as I made it sound. I mean, I could be moving faster. But I mean everything I worked on is still there. Websites don't burn.

MARY All right.

BEN I'll do whatever you want. We can do whatever.

MARY Well, we have the car. (BEN *and* MARY *look at the remains of the house.* MARY *speaks to* BEN) I think I dreamt about the people in the next room in the Super 8. I dreamt that they were wizards. Cooking something up for us in a big cauldron.

BEN Did they reach in and pull out a new house?

MARY One of them ladled out a cup for me, and right before I took a sip, I thought, "Oh, right. This is my closure dream." (*does* MARY *take* BEN*'s hand?*)

They were loading up their suitcases this morning when I went down to the 7-Eleven for coffee. They drove away in an old station wagon.

BEN Only two of them. The other two stayed. They were watching *Good Morning America* when I left. I saw them through the window.

MARY Who knows who they are. They could be anybody, really.

BEN *puts his arms around* MARY. *They look at the remains of their burned-down house.*

Blackout.

ADDENDUM

To produce the play set in two backyards (instead of back and front), please make the following changes:

SCENE 2

Mary should not enter the scene from her house. It should seem as though she sneaked out the front door of her house and has been roaming around the neighborhood.

Also, if the show is set in the two backyards, there should be an obviously fake plant near Sharon and Kenny's back door through the whole show.

SCENE 4

On page 55, at the end of Sharon's dog rant, change "And she just shook her head and kind of kicked our plant and said, 'Ha, I thought it was fake'" to "And she just shook her head and turned and jogged away."

SCENE 6

On page 68, cut from "I think this might be against the law" through "Shit then, private property" and INSERT the following exchange, after Kenny says "I'm an asshole, and it's too late for me"

KENNY (*looks at* BEN's *house*) Look at that house.

BEN What about it?

KENNY You own that house!

BEN Yeah, well, I mean the bank owns it.

Then go right to Kenny's "You gotta hang on to that house, Ben." And continue the scene as written.